CRYPTOCURRENCY APPS FOR BUDGETING BLOCKCHAIN & MORE

Managing The Digital Economy For Security And Wealth Creation

WealthWise by M. Finley

Cryptocurrency, Apps for Budgeting, Blockchain, & More

Managing The Digital Economy For Security And Wealth Creation

©WealthWise by M. Finley, 2024.

Table Of Content

Chapter 1: The Revolution in Digital Finance

Chapter 2: Using Apps to Manage Your Budget

Chapter 3: Handling Investments in Cryptocurrencies

Chapter 4: Leveraging the Potential of Online Banking

Chapter 5: Investing in the Digital Economy

Chapter 6: Safeguarding Your Electronic Resources

Chapter 7: Making Future Plans

Copyright

All rights reserved for all works, places, events and incidents are written by me and cannot be produced, stored or even translated without my permission. This includes a part, a screenshot or anything as long as it is part of my work.

Copyright **WealthWise by M. Finley, 2024.**

Disclaimer

The information provided in this book is for educational and informational purposes only. While every effort has been made to ensure the accuracy and reliability of the content, the author and publisher make no warranties or guarantees regarding the completeness, suitability, or applicability of the information presented. Readers are advised to conduct their own research and consult with financial professionals before making any investment or financial decisions. The author and publisher shall not be liable for any losses, damages, or consequences arising from the use of the information provided in this book.

Cryptocurrency is at the forefront of the decentralisation revolution, which is taking place in real time and bringing about a more transparent and equal financial system.

One transaction at a time, budgeting applications serve as our compasses, leading us towards financial empowerment and control. They are more than just tools.

Beyond the purview of conventional banking is a world of limitless opportunities, where innovation powers our ascent to prosperity and financial freedom.

Odyssey of Digital Finance

The field of personal finance has experienced significant change in an era characterized by quickening technology innovation and digital revolution. The days of reconciling cheque books and going to physical banks are long gone; these days, our financial life is becoming more and more entwined with the internet. Our approach to managing, investing, and growing our finances has been completely transformed by technology, from the emergence of cryptocurrencies to the widespread use of budgeting applications and more.

This is "**Cryptocurrency, Apps for Budgeting, Blockchain, & More:** Your Roadmap to Financial Freedom." We take a tour around the digital economy in these pages, looking at the instruments, fads, and tactics that influence the contemporary financial scene. This book is your road map to realising the full potential of the digital age, whether you're an experienced investor looking for fresh opportunities or a beginner figuring out the ins and outs of personal finance for the first time.

Come along as we explore the world of cryptocurrencies, where blockchain technology and digital assets have the potential to completely change the way we perceive money.

We'll explain the complexities of this quickly changing market, from Bitcoin to Ethereum and beyond, enabling you to understand the potential and hazards of the cryptocurrency environment and make wise investment decisions.

However, our adventure doesn't end there. We'll also talk about how budgeting apps may change people's lives by giving them unmatched access to their financial information and control. These digital tools are essential allies on the journey to financial empowerment, helping with everything from tracking expenditure to creating savings objectives and streamlining spending patterns.

However, as we continue to explore the digital frontier, we will come across a wide range of opportunities and difficulties that go beyond the domains of cryptocurrencies, budgeting apps, blockchain technology, and more. Our investigation of the digital economy will cover the entire range of potential avenues for accumulating wealth and safeguarding our financial futures, from the digitization of banking services to the introduction of fresh investment opportunities and the constant necessity of financial security.

Thus, **"Cryptocurrency, Apps for Budgeting, Blockchain, & More"** is your road map to financial independence in the digital age, regardless of your desire to investigate the possibilities of cryptocurrencies, leverage the strength of budgeting apps, or venture into unexplored lands of the digital economy. Come along with me as we set out on this life-changing adventure.

Chapter 1: The Revolution in Digital Finance

The digital financial revolution has had a greater impact than few other periods in economic history. The advent of online banking and the growth of fintech technologies are only two examples of how the relentless march of technology has fundamentally altered the landscape of personal finance.

This first chapter takes us on a historical journey, charting the origins of the financial revolution that was brought about by digital means and analysing the significant transformations that have changed the way we manage and connect to money. We examine the key moments in history that brought about the digital age of money, including the development of mobile banking and the internet.

But as much as it is a story of technological growth, the digital financial revolution is also one of democratisation and empowerment. Financial services are becoming more accessible and inclusive, giving people from all walks of life previously unheard-of possibilities to take control of their financial destinies and build better lives for themselves and their families.

Join us as we unravel the threads of this digital tapestry, illuminating the transformative potential of the digital financial revolution and setting the stage for our exploration of the fascinating new domains of cryptocurrency, budgeting software, and other associated subjects.

The personal finance industry has seen a radical transformation with the advent of technology. From the early days of online banking to the rapid expansion of fintech companies, technology has had a profound impact on how we handle, access, and interact with our money.

The journey began with the development of online banking, a revolutionary concept that converted traditional banking into a digital setting. People could now complete their banking transactions from the comfort of their homes or workplaces with a few mouse clicks or taps on a smartphone screen, bidding adieu to the days of long lines and paper-based transactions. This improved convenience, which also saves time and effort, has made banking more efficient and convenient for millions of individuals worldwide.

But online banking was only the beginning. As technology advanced at an exponential rate, so did the scope and complexity of fintech concepts. From peer-to-peer payment systems that facilitated easy transactions between individuals to mobile banking applications that allowed users to manage their accounts while on the go, fintech companies completely reshaped the financial services industry.

One of the most notable recent developments is the rise of robo-advisors, which are algorithmic platforms offering automated financial advising and portfolio management services. By utilising cutting-edge algorithms and data analytics, these robo-advisors are able to offer customised investment plans that are based on each person's unique financial goals, risk tolerance, and time horizon. This democratisation of investing advice has empowered people from all walks of life to take control of their financial futures and make confident decisions without the need for costly human financial counsellors.

Furthermore, the advancement of machine learning and artificial intelligence technologies has opened up new avenues for personal finance research. Solutions driven by artificial intelligence (AI) are revolutionising the way we manage our finances and make informed financial decisions. Predictive analytics systems that identify investment possibilities and forecast market trends, as well as intelligent chatbots that offer prompt customer support, are some examples of these technologies.

In summary, technology has significantly changed how individuals handle their personal finances. The advent of internet banking and the rise of fintech innovations have allowed people to handle their accounts like never before. As we continue to embrace the digital revolution, personal finance appears to be more powerful, accessible, and effective than it has ever been.

The use of digital financial instruments represents a significant paradigm shift in the way that individuals manage their finances; there are several benefits as well as a number of challenges that need be properly evaluated. In this inquiry, we delve into the intricate realm of virtual currency, examining both the advantages of convenience and accessibility in addition to the pressing security concerns that accompany this swift progress in technology.

At the vanguard of this shift is the remarkable convenience that digital banking provides for customers in managing their financial affairs. Thanks to digital technologies, customers may now conduct a range of financial activities with unparalleled speed and efficiency. Gone are the days of tedious paperwork and long lineups at physical banks. People can utilise digital financial tools to manage their finances anytime, anywhere. These tools allow users to perform things like paying bills, transferring money between accounts, and monitoring investment portfolios with a few mouse clicks or smartphone touches.

Additionally, the accessibility of digital financial instruments has greatly increased, reducing barriers and promoting financial inclusion for individuals worldwide. In places where access to traditional banking infrastructure is limited or nonexistent, digital platforms act as a lifeline, providing people with essential financial services including savings accounts, loans, and payment methods. This enhanced accessibility not only helps marginalised populations participate more fully in the global economy, but it also fosters economic growth and development on a larger scale.

However, there are a lot of disadvantages to digital money as well, the biggest of which are security concerns. As more and more financial transactions move online, customers must contend with cybersecurity risks such as data breaches, identity theft, and financial fraud, to name just a few. Cybercriminals constantly adapt their tactics and employ cutting-edge techniques to gain access to digital networks and pilfer sensitive financial information. Therefore, it is imperative to ensure the security and integrity of digital financial transactions. To do this, financial institutions and individual users must continue to pay close attention to cybersecurity threats and implement stringent authentication protocols.

Concerns have also been raised regarding consumer protection and regulatory compliance because the digital banking industry is seeing rapid technological innovation at a rate that may occasionally outpace regulatory oversight. Current regulatory frameworks need to be modified by policymakers to address emerging risks and safeguard consumer interests as digital financial instruments continue to grow and proliferate. To find the right balance between fostering innovation and protecting consumers, governments, regulatory agencies, financial institutions, and technology companies must collaborate to develop effective regulatory frameworks that enable innovation while minimising any risks.

In conclusion, the unparalleled accessibility and simplicity offered by digital financial instruments revolutionise personal financial management and promote financial inclusion on a worldwide scale. However, the widespread adoption of digital banking presents significant security challenges that must be addressed to avert cyberattacks and maintain client welfare. By strengthening regulatory oversight, promoting stakeholder participation, and implementing robust cybersecurity measures, we can reduce the risks connected with digital banking while optimising its revolutionary potential. Everyone will benefit from the financial ecosystem becoming safer and more robust as a result.

Chapter 2: Using Apps to Manage Your Budget

Having instant access to financial management tools through a plethora of budgeting programmes has made it easier than ever for people to comprehend personal finance in the digital era. In this chapter, we go into the world of budgeting apps, exploring their potentially revolutionary potential and provide guidance on how individuals can use these useful tools to take financial control and achieve their goals.

Rather than just tracking expenses and writing checks, learning how to utilise budgeting apps efficiently is truly about cultivating an attitude of financial empowerment and awareness. Users can easily manage their income, monitor their expenses, and set savings goals with the help of budgeting apps, which give them a complete view of their financial status. By giving users real-time insights into their financial behaviours and patterns, these programmes help users make informed financial decisions, identify areas for improvement, and progressively form healthy financial habits.

Furthermore, budgeting software offer a level of personalisation and versatility that traditional budgeting strategies just cannot equal. Users can personalise everything about their budgeting experience, from spending category personalisation to goal and notification customisation, to meet their own needs and interests. Whether they are tracking erratic income sources, setting money aside for a particular objective, or creating a monthly budget, budgeting apps give users the resources and adaptability they need to meet their unique financial circumstances.

Setting objectives and tracking advancement are two of the most useful features of budgeting software. Budgeting apps allow users to set and track specific financial objectives, such as paying off debt, saving for a down payment on a house, or creating an emergency fund. By tracking their progress and celebrating small victories along the way, users are motivated to stay on course and keep moving in the direction of achieving their financial goals.

However, there are some challenges involved in picking up the use of budgeting software. Maintaining a regular and diligent use of the app is one of the most common issues that users encounter. Like any habit, effective budgeting takes time, effort, and consistency, therefore users might find it challenging to continue using the app over time. Additionally, users could have UI issues or technical challenges that limit their ability to fully utilise the app's features and functionalities.

Furthermore, as budgeting apps are only as good as the data they get, users need to be careful to accurately enter and categorise their financial actions in order to gain insightful knowledge from them. If this isn't done, the app's value as a financial management tool will be diminished due to erroneous budgeting calculations and skewed financial reporting.

In conclusion, mastering the usage of budgeting software is an excellent way to take control of your finances and accomplish your financial goals. The data and tools provided by budgeting programmes allow users to track their progress towards their goals, create healthier financial habits, and ultimately achieve greater financial stability and independence. However, mastery of budgeting software necessitates commitment, consistency, and meticulousness. Users must also be prepared to get over obstacles and setbacks. If one is dedicated and persistent, mastering budgeting software could be a game-changer for a more optimistic financial future.

Taking a look at budgeting tools and applications is like embarking on a journey towards empowerment and financial control. With the aim of streamlining the budgeting process, monitoring spending, establishing savings objectives, and efficiently managing budgets, these digital tools provide users with an abundance of features and functionalities. Based on individual needs and interests, we provide recommendations for the best budgeting tool in this analysis, empowering users to take charge of their money and maximise the benefits of budgeting software.

Being aware of the variety of options available is the first step towards delving into the world of budgeting apps. Users can choose from a wide range of personal finance platforms and specialised budgeting apps to find the perfect tool for their financial needs. The usability, compatibility with existing bank accounts, capabilities offered, and cost structure are important factors to take into account while evaluating budgeting software. By carefully weighing these factors, users are able to focus their search results and identify budgeting programmes that align with their personal goals and preferences.

Once users have identified potential budgeting applications, the next step is to evaluate the features and capabilities of each app to determine which one best meets their needs. To categorise and monitor their spending habits in real time, users should, at the very least, look for budgeting apps that have expense tracking features. The goal-setting features of budgeting applications, which let users establish savings targets and track their progress over time, might also be something to consider. Other useful features to look out for are bill tracking, debt management tools, and personalised budgeting categories.

Additionally, users should examine how much automation and integration budgeting apps provide, since this can greatly expedite the budgeting process and improve user experience.

Users can save a lot of time and effort by using budgeting apps that provide automatic transaction categorization, real-time account syncing, integration with financial institutions, and other services. This way, users can concentrate on reaching their financial objectives rather than handling time-consuming administrative tasks.

Users should assess the security and privacy measures taken by budgeting apps to protect sensitive financial data in addition to examining features and functioning. Look for budgeting programmes that use encryption protocols, multi-factor authentication, and robust security measures to shield user data from online threats and illegal access. It's possible to learn a lot about budgeting software providers' commitment to security and customer privacy by reading user reviews and looking up their reputation and track record.

In conclusion, stepping into the realm of budgeting applications provides users a great tool for taking control of their money and accomplishing their financial objectives. Users can speed up the budgeting process, monitor expenses, set savings goals, and manage budgets with confidence and ease by carefully weighing their options, selecting the best budgeting programme, and effectively utilising all of its features. Using the right guidance and approach, budgeting apps could be useful allies on the road to financial control and empowerment.

It could be challenging to navigate the sea of budgeting apps because there are so many of them vying for users' attention and time. To help readers make wise decisions, it's important to examine the features, prices, and user experiences of some of the top budgeting applications available. By providing a comprehensive analysis of these leading rivals, readers may gain valuable insight into the benefits and drawbacks of each app, empowering them to select the ideal one for their own needs and preferences.

Mint's vast feature set and user-friendly design make it one of the most popular budgeting apps out there. Users may link their bank accounts, monitor their spending, set savings goals, and create personalized budgets using Mint that fit their unique requirements and preferences. With its automated transaction categorization and real-time updates, Mint provides users with a clear and accurate picture of their financial status, empowering them to make informed decisions and adhere to their budgets. People with different financial backgrounds can use Mint because it is free.

Another major player in the budgeting app market is **YNAB (You Need a Budget),** which is renowned for its proactive approach to budgeting and emphasis on zero-based budgeting concepts. Every dollar should be allocated to a specific category by YNAB members in order to guarantee total accountability and openness in their spending habits. YNAB offers a comprehensive system with features including goal monitoring, debt repayment tools, live classes, and support for individuals who want to manage their finances. YNAB's price approach entails a monthly or annual subscription fee.

Customers who want a more active approach to budgeting can use EveryDollar as a straightforward yet effective option. EveryDollar allows users to allocate every dollar to a specific category and track their spending in real-time by employing the zero-based budgeting method.

EveryDollar provides users with the tools necessary to meet their financial goals, such as adjustable budget categories, transaction tracking, and debt payback options. There are two price categories for EveryDollar: a free basic version and a premium version with additional features and support.

In addition to the top applications described above, there are many other budgeting apps that should be considered, each with unique features and benefits. For example, because Personal Capital offers extensive retirement planning and investment monitoring tools in addition to its budgeting capabilities, it is a popular choice among users who want to manage their assets and money on a single platform. **PocketGuard** gives customers a clear view of their financial situation and helpful guidance on how to improve their spending habits, with a focus on simplifying budgeting and cost tracking.

The best budgeting tool for any individual will ultimately depend on their unique needs, preferences, and financial goals. Comparing the features, prices, and user experiences of each top-rated budgeting programme can provide readers with crucial insights into the benefits and drawbacks of each. They will be able to select the most effective tool to help them achieve financial achievement thanks to this. It's crucial to select a budgeting programme, such as Mint, YNAB, EveryDollar, or another great choice, that matches your specific financial situation and provides you with the ease and confidence to manage your finances.

Chapter 3: Handling Investments in Cryptocurrencies

Few things in the quickly changing world of finance have intrigued and captivated investors' attention as much as cryptocurrencies. This chapter takes readers on a tour of the world of cryptocurrency investing, examining the advantages and disadvantages of this new asset class.

Cryptocurrency is essentially a digital money that runs without the help of central authorities or conventional financial institutions, relying instead on encryption for security. Since its 2009 debut, dozens of additional digital assets—each with distinct characteristics and applications—have joined the ranks of Bitcoin, the first and most well-known cryptocurrency.

The opportunity to earn enormous profits is one of the main draws of investing in cryptocurrencies. For astute investors and early adopters, cryptocurrencies have produced astounding returns over the last ten years, with certain assets seeing exponential value rise. But there is a significant risk associated with the possibility of huge gains, and cryptocurrency markets are infamous for their volatility and unpredictability. Risk management techniques, a thorough grasp of market dynamics, and the capacity to tolerate large swings in asset values are all necessary for navigating bitcoin investments.

Furthermore, inexperienced investors may find it daunting due to the bitcoin landscape's immense variety and complexity. Choosing the proper investments involves rigorous study and due diligence since there are hundreds of digital assets to pick from, each with its own distinct features, use cases, and underlying technology. To find attractive investment possibilities and reduce possible dangers, investors must evaluate elements like market liquidity, adoption potential, development activity, and regulatory issues.

Furthermore, managing bitcoin investments requires a thorough comprehension of the guiding concepts and underlying technologies of these virtual assets. The majority of cryptocurrencies are built on distributed ledger technology, or blockchain, which is essential to maintaining transaction security, immutability, and transparency. For investors to appropriately assess the long-term feasibility and potential of cryptocurrency investments, they need to understand the basics of blockchain technology.

Handling legal and compliance issues is necessary while handling cryptocurrency investments, in addition to market dynamics and technical factors. The legal landscape around cryptocurrency exchanges is quickly changing, and governments and regulatory agencies worldwide are having difficulty adequately categorizing and controlling digital assets. To protect themselves from legal and financial risks, investors need to be aware of regulatory changes in their countries and make sure that relevant rules and regulations are followed.

In summary, investors looking to get exposure to this new asset class have both possibilities and obstacles while handling cryptocurrency investing. The cryptocurrency markets are marked by volatility, complexity, and regulatory uncertainty despite the evident potential for large rewards. Investors who want to effectively handle bitcoin investments need to do their homework, be cautious, and use good risk management techniques. Through cautious, long-term thinking, and care when investing in cryptocurrencies, investors may benefit from this innovative technology's transformational potential while reducing associated dangers.

Deciphering the cryptocurrency world is necessary before appreciating this new asset class's revolutionary potential. In this study, we offer a comprehensive examination of three of the most well-known digital assets: Bitcoin, Ethereum, and Litecoin. We want to make clear each cryptocurrency's significance in relation to the broader context of digital money by analysing its unique features, uses, and underlying technology.

The 2009 release of the Bitcoin whitepaper, commonly recognised as the first cryptocurrency, was credited to an anonymous individual or group going by the name Satoshi Nakamoto. The decentralised network of nodes that makes up Bitcoin uses the blockchain, a public ledger, to record and validate transactions. Coined "digital gold" due to its rarity, security, and value retention, Bitcoin was the first cryptocurrency to become widely accepted. Due to its limited number of 21 million coins, Bitcoin has become more and more well-known as a potential replacement for traditional fiat money and as an inflation hedge.

Ethereum, a platform for decentralised apps (dApps) and smart contracts, was introduced in 2015 by programmer Vitalik Buterin and represents a significant advancement in blockchain technology. Unlike Bitcoin, which is primarily used as a digital currency, Ethereum enables developers to create and implement decentralised apps that run on its blockchain. In addition to serving as a medium of exchange, Ether (ETH), the native cryptocurrency of the Ethereum network, powers the execution of smart contracts. Because of its programmability and flexibility, Ethereum is a leading platform for blockchain innovation and experimentation. As a result, it has been widely adopted in several sectors, such as decentralised finance (DeFi), non-fungible tokens (NFTs), and decentralised autonomous organisations (DAOs).

Litecoin is frequently referred to as the "silver to Bitcoin's gold." Charlie Lee, a former Google programmer, launched the cryptocurrency in 2011. Litecoin shares several characteristics with Bitcoin, including a proof-of-work consensus mechanism and a supply model driven by scarcity. However, Litecoin distinguishes itself with its faster block generation time and lower transaction costs, making it a more sensible and cost-effective means of exchange for regular transactions. Even though Litecoin may not have gained as much traction as Bitcoin or Ethereum, it is still a popular choice for cryptocurrency fans and merchants searching for a stable and convenient digital currency.

Apart from Bitcoin, Ethereum, and Litecoin, a plethora of other digital assets are also available, each with distinct characteristics, applications, and value propositions. The cryptocurrency market is full of unique and inventive coins, ranging from platform tokens like Binance Coin and Cardano to privacy-focused coins like Monero and Zcash. Through grasping the foundations of well-known digital assets such as Bitcoin, Ethereum, and Litecoin, enthusiasts and investors can gain essential understanding of the broader cryptocurrency landscape and put themselves in a position to benefit from the disruptive technology's revolutionary potential.

If cryptocurrencies gain more traction and widespread acceptance, they have the potential to fundamentally impact not just the financial sector but also a variety of other industries, such as supply chain management, healthcare, and digital identity verification. Blockchain technology, which offers a transparent and secure framework for recording and validating transactions, is the cornerstone upon which the majority of cryptocurrencies are constructed. As a result, its applications are not limited to banking.

Blockchain-based voting systems, decentralised finance (DeFi) platforms, and non-fungible tokens (NFTs) are just a few examples of the innovations that are transforming traditional businesses and procedures with the help of cryptocurrencies and blockchain technology.

These developments demonstrate how revolutionary cryptocurrencies could be in terms of empowering individuals to take control of their digital assets and identities, democratising access to financial services, and promoting accountability and transparency.

But in order to fully use cryptocurrencies, a number of issues must be resolved, such as scalability, interoperability, and regulatory compliance. The widespread use of cryptocurrencies for regular transactions may be hampered by scalability problems including high transaction costs and network congestion. Interoperability issues could make it more challenging for assets and data to move between platforms without any problems, such as incompatibilities and a lack of standardisation between different blockchain networks.

Furthermore, governments and regulatory organizations throughout the globe are struggling to properly categorize and control digital assets, which presents major challenges for cryptocurrency projects and users in addition to regulatory uncertainties and compliance needs. For the bitcoin ecosystem to be competitive and sustainable over the long haul, it is vital to strike the optimal balance between fostering innovation and defending consumer interests.

To sum up, cryptocurrencies such as Bitcoin, Ethereum, and Litecoin indicate a huge paradigm change in the way we view and use money and technology. Through analysing the universe of cryptocurrencies and appreciating its different qualities, applications, and difficulties, investors and enthusiasts may adeptly and tactically traverse the fast shifting terrain of digital finance. Cryptocurrencies have the opportunity to bring in a new age of financial inclusion, innovation, and empowerment for people and communities throughout the globe with continued invention, cooperation, and regulatory clarity.

While cryptocurrency investing can be extremely rewarding, there are risks and challenges associated with it as well. To assist you make informed bitcoin investments, consider the following useful advice:

1. **Educate Yourself:** Before making any investments, take the time to get knowledgeable about the technology, the workings of the market, and the risks related to cryptocurrencies. Acquaint yourself with the many types of digital assets that are available, their functions, and the factors influencing their cost.

2. **Increase the Size of Your Portfolio:** Diversification is key to risk management in all investment types. Rather of investing all of your money in a single cryptocurrency, consider spreading your portfolio among several assets to distribute risk and minimise potential losses.

3. **Invest Just Enough to Lose:** Due to their tremendous volatility, the price of cryptocurrencies can fluctuate dramatically over brief periods of time. Only make investments with money you can afford to lose if it doesn't affect your long-term financial objectives or stability.

4. **Set Reasonable Objectives and Expectations:** Indicate your objectives for your investments in clear terms, together with your realistic expectations for returns. Understand that there is some risk involved in investing in cryptocurrencies, and that results may not always be favourable.

5. **Employ Dollar-Cost Averaging (DCA):** Rather than trying to time the market, use a dollar-cost averaging approach to gradually invest a particular amount of money at regular periods, regardless of market swings. This approach could help to balance out price volatility and reduce

the likelihood of making snap decisions when investing.

6. **Employ Risk Management Strategies:** Consider utilising risk management strategies, such as stop-loss orders, to minimise potential losses and protect profits. By following your investment plan and establishing exit points, you can mitigate market downturns.

7. **Safeguard Your Financial Assets:** Prioritise security by utilising reliable cryptocurrency wallets and exchanges, securing your recovery phrases and private keys, coming up with secure passwords, and utilising two-factor authentication (2FA). Avoid visiting questionable websites or applications, con artists, and phishing scams.

8. **Keep Up with Regulation Changes:** Keep abreast of the regulations in your jurisdiction and the requirements for

compliance. Understand the potential tax and legal repercussions of cryptocurrency investing, and make sure you comply with all applicable rules and laws.

9. **<u>Regularly Monitor Your Investments:</u>** Keep tabs on your cryptocurrency holdings and stay up to date on news, trends, and developments that could affect prices. Use tools and resources for portfolio monitoring to keep an eye on the performance of your investments and make wise decisions.

10. **<u>Seek Expert Advice if Needed:</u>** Based on your particular situation and risk tolerance, financial advisors and cryptocurrency specialists can provide tailored advice. Consider asking them for advice if you're unclear of how to invest in cryptocurrencies responsibly or if you require specific direction.

You can make ethical cryptocurrency investments and deal with the complexities of the digital asset market with more security and confidence if you adhere to these useful advice and tactics. Recall to remain knowledgeable, alert, and methodical when it comes to investing in cryptocurrencies.

Chapter 4: Leveraging the Potential of Online Banking

The world is becoming more and more digital, and as a result, traditional banking is changing drastically. Digital banking is becoming a major factor in financial services innovation and convenience. This chapter looks at how online banking came to be and all the benefits it offers to businesses and consumers.

The phrase "digital banking" refers to a broad category of online and mobile financial services that enable users to conveniently manage their accounts, conduct transactions, and access banking services from any location at any time. People's interactions with their funds have fundamentally changed as a result of digital banking's unparalleled accessibility, efficiency, and ease. Online account management tools and mobile banking apps are a couple of examples of these platforms.

One of the key advantages of digital banking is the capacity to do an array of financial procedures without the need to physically visit a branch. Digital banking provides consumers with the ease and convenience to manage their finances through services like bill payment, account monitoring, mobile check deposit, and fund transfers. With digital banking, clients have direct access to financial management tools, which save time and streamline typical banking tasks. These options include real-time cash transfers between accounts, bill payment by smartphone, and account balance monitoring while on the go.

Furthermore, the greater accessibility of digital banking might help people who might not have easy access to traditional financial services, such as those who live in underprivileged neighbourhoods or rural locations. By removing geographic restrictions and improving accessibility to financial services through digital channels, digital banking promotes financial inclusion and helps people participate more fully in the global economy.

Digital banking also enables financial institutions to leverage analytics and data-driven insights to offer targeted and customised services to their customers. Banks can use consumer data and behaviour patterns to tailor their services to the unique needs and preferences of each individual user. This enhances client loyalty and the overall banking experience.

To fully reap the rewards of digital banking, however, a number of challenges must be addressed, including cybersecurity risks, privacy concerns, and regulatory compliance. The increasing trend of digital banking transactions being conducted through online and mobile platforms exposes consumers to a variety of cybersecurity dangers, including phishing scams, malware attacks, and data breaches. Financial institutions must spend heavily in robust cybersecurity solutions and best practices to protect sensitive client data from fraudulent activity and unauthorised access.

In addition, privacy concerns raise serious ethical and legal issues with the collection and use of customer data in digital banking transactions. To protect consumer privacy rights and uphold confidence in digital banking services, financial institutions must provide transparency and accountability in their data handling operations, obtain consumers' informed consent, and adhere to applicable privacy laws and regulations.

In summary, taking advantage of digital banking's potential offers a host of benefits and opportunities for individuals, businesses, and financial institutions. Financial institutions can enhance customer engagement, create operational efficiencies, and encourage financial inclusion by incorporating digital banking technologies and innovations. Customers may benefit from enhanced comfort, accessibility, and efficiency when managing their accounts. To ensure that digital banking services continue to be safe, transparent, and compliant with current laws and regulations, it is necessary to address cybersecurity threats, privacy concerns, and regulatory barriers in order to fully realise the potential of digital banking.

Online and mobile banking programmes, which offer a multitude of features and functionalities that promote efficiency, accessibility, and convenience, have radically changed the way individuals handle their money. Let's examine some of the primary benefits of these online banking services, like mobile cheque deposit, real-time account monitoring, and bill payment:

1. **Mobile Check Deposit:** By allowing users to deposit checks into their bank accounts using their smartphones or tablets, this service removes the need for clients to physically visit a bank branch or ATM. To use mobile check deposits, users only need to take a picture of the front and back of the check, enter the desired amount, and send it electronically through the banking app. This feature saves time and effort by enabling clients to quickly and safely deposit checks from anywhere at any time without having to visit the bank or wait in line.

2. **Bill Pay:** Customers can pay their invoices online directly from their bank accounts thanks to convenient bill pay features. Both mobile banking apps and internet banking offer these choices. The ease of using electronic devices allows consumers to schedule one-time or recurring bill payments, monitor payment history, and do much more. Bill pay features give customers greater financial independence and control, speed up the bill payment process, and reduce the possibility of missing or late payments.

3. **Real-Time Account Monitoring:** One of the main benefits of online and mobile banking is the ability to monitor account activity in real-time. Users can track transactions, check account balances, and receive real-time notifications for account-related activity including low balances, withdrawals, and deposits. Customers may monitor their financial status, detect fraudulent or unauthorized

activity promptly, and take proactive measures to manage their money wisely with real-time account monitoring.

4. **Transfer Funds:** Through online and mobile banking apps, users can transfer funds between accounts at the same bank as well as to external accounts at other financial institutions. Whether transferring funds between checking and savings accounts, mailing money to friends and family, or making loan payments, users may quickly and securely start transferring using the banking app. Customers may move money more quickly and efficiently to meet their needs with the use of the transfer funds tool, all without giving up freedom or control over their accounts.

5. **Access to Account Statements and Documents:** Online and mobile banking services make it simple for users to access account statements, documents, and

transaction history. Since users can read and download account statements, tax documents, and transaction history directly from the banking app, paper statements are no longer required, which also reduces clutter. With access to account statements and supporting paperwork, users may track their financial history, reconcile transactions, and maintain correct records for tax and budgetary purposes.

All things considered, internet and mobile banking offer a plethora of benefits that empower users to manage their money, handle their accounts, and conduct financial transactions with ease. These digital banking capabilities, which include features like bill payment, fund transfers, real-time account monitoring, access to account statements and documents, and mobile cheque deposit, have become essential for managing finances in the modern world.

There are several concerns concerning online banking security, which must be addressed in order to reassure clients and ensure the security of their personal information. When utilising online banking, the following tips will assist safeguard confidential information and prevent identity theft:

1. **<u>Choose Robust Passwords:</u>** Ensure that the passwords on your online bank accounts are strong, unique, and challenging to decipher. Use of names or dates of birth is prohibited. Use a password manager and make sure your passwords contain a mix of letters, numbers, and special characters in order to securely store and manage your passwords.

2. **<u>Activate Two-Factor Authentication (2FA):</u>** Set up two-factor authentication (2FA) for your online bank accounts whenever it is possible. 2FA adds an extra degree of security by requiring a second

form of verification in addition to your password, such as a code sent to your mobile device or generated by an authenticator app.

3. **Maintain Software Updates:** Update your computer, smartphone, and banking software on a regular basis to ensure you have the most recent security patches and updates installed. Cybercriminals may get unauthorised access to your device or data by taking advantage of security flaws in out-of-date software.

4. **Phishing scams:** Avoid answering unwanted calls, messages, or emails requesting personal information, or allowing them to convince you to click on suspicious links or open attachments. Phishing tactics are frequently used by cybercriminals to fool victims into disclosing personal information or to allow malware to infiltrate their computers.

5. **Use Secure Wi-Fi Networks:** Avoid doing online banking transactions on public Wi-Fi networks as they could be unreliable and open to eavesdropping by hackers. Use a secure, password-protected Wi-Fi network or a virtual private network (VPN) to protect your data and encrypt your internet connection.

6. **Watch Account Behaviour:** Regularly monitor your online banking accounts for any odd or suspicious activity, such as unauthorised transactions or changes to account settings. Please report any discrepancies or issues to your bank as soon as possible. You may also want to consider setting up account notifications for added security.

7. **Protect Your Devices:** To keep your computer, smartphone, and other devices safe, make use of firewalls, security features, and the most latest antivirus

software. Enable device encryption and biometric authentication (such as fingerprint or face recognition) to provide an extra degree of protection against unauthorized access.

8. **Be Wary of Public Computers:** Avoid accessing your online banking accounts on shared or public computers since they may be compromised or infected with malware. If you must use a public computer, be sure to completely log out of all of your accounts and clear your browsing history and cache after each session.

9. **Examine Privacy Settings:** Check the security features and privacy settings offered by your bank's online banking platform, and make any required changes to enhance the security of your account. Consider minimizing the personal information you share on the internet and

decline to take part in any projects that require the sharing of unnecessary data.

10. **Remain Informed and Vigilant:** When making purchases online, stay vigilant by staying informed on the latest security threats and advised procedures for online banking safety. Trust your instincts and exercise caution if something looks suspicious or too good to be true.

By following these guidelines and taking preventative security precautions, you may safeguard your personal data and prevent identity theft when using online banking. Remember to protect your assets and financial data from internet threats by being vigilant, informed, and proactive.

Chapter 5: Investing in the Digital Economy

With its revolutionary impact on investing paradigms and plenty of lucrative opportunities for investors, the digital economy has emerged as a significant force in the modern era. This chapter delves into the intricate realm of investing in the digital economy, elucidating the novel trends, intricate dynamics, and strategic prerequisites that facilitate prosperity in this swiftly evolving milieu.

1. **Dynamics of the Digital Economy:** A wide range of industries, from well-established technology corporations to up-and-coming disruptors, are included in the digital economy due to their mutual reliance on digital platforms and technologies. This networked ecosystem fosters creativity, efficiency, and

scalability, driving exponential development and transforming global industries. A thorough understanding of the fundamental mechanics of the digital economy is essential for investors hoping to capitalize on its transformative potential.

2. **Emerging trends:** A number of advances in the digital economy are providing appealing growth opportunities and altering the way investments are made. E-commerce has expanded quickly as a result of changing consumer preferences and the increasing use of online purchasing, creating new investment opportunities in digital marketplaces, transportation infrastructure, and retail technology. Moreover, the expansion of cloud computing, artificial intelligence, and data analytics is stimulating innovation in a number of industries, such as corporate software and healthcare. Investors need to keep a watch on these

new developments in order to identify high-growth industries and businesses positioned for success in the digital economy.

3. **Important industries:** The digital economy comprises a wide range of industries, each with unique investment potential and risk profiles. Technology is at the core of digital investment, with opportunities in semiconductors, telecommunications, hardware, and software. Fintech, or financial technology, is another new sector of the economy. With the aid of innovations like digital wallets, mobile banking, and blockchain technology, fintech is revolutionizing traditional banking and payment methods. Other innovative businesses that are transforming industries include cybersecurity, e-commerce, digital entertainment, and the Internet of Things (IoT).

4. **Success Strategies:** To successfully traverse the complexities of investing in the digital economy, a methodical approach based on in-depth research, risk assessment, and diversification is required. Investors must conduct extensive due diligence in order to evaluate the fundamentals of potential investments, including market dynamics, competitive positioning, development opportunities, and management quality. Furthermore, diversifying across businesses and asset classes can help minimize risk and maximize rewards in the dynamic and oftentimes unpredictable digital economy. Furthermore, maintaining a long-term view and staying up to date with technical advancements and market trends are necessary for identifying opportunities and adapting to shifting market conditions.

5. **Risk factors:** Despite the digital economy's enormous development

potential, investing in it entails considerable risk. Investors face numerous risks in this dynamic environment, including volatility, unpredictable regulations, disruptive competition, and cybersecurity concerns. Thorough risk assessments and risk management strategies need to be implemented in order to safeguard investments and preserve capital in the face of unpredictability.

In conclusion, there are many prospects for investors in the digital economy who want to learn about cutting-edge technologies and rapidly expanding sectors of the economy. Understanding the dynamics, trends, and industries driving the digital economy and applying a scientific and strategic approach to investing can help investors position themselves to capitalise on the huge potential of this dynamic and rapidly changing world.

Investing in technology companies, online marketplaces, and emerging industries like blockchain and artificial intelligence (AI) carries both risks and rewards. Let's take a closer look at each:

1. **Prospects:**

A. Innovation and disruption: Technology companies and emerging industries are leading the way in innovation and upending many different sectors. By making an investment in these companies, you may take advantage of cutting-edge technology and ground-breaking business ideas that have the potential to transform whole industries and provide significant returns.

B. Growth Potential: Technology companies, particularly those in fast-growing sectors like cloud computing, blockchain, and artificial intelligence, have a lot of potential to grow. These companies' development trajectory is ascribed to the quick advancement of technology, increased market opportunities, and growing adoption rates. These businesses are thus ideal investment choices for those looking for long-term capital gains.

C. Scalability and Efficiency: Companies that depend on digital platforms and technology frequently benefit from economies of scale and operational efficiency, which can spur growth and income. Platforms may expand rapidly and gain market share because of network effects, automation, and data analytics, which also produce long-term competitive advantages and riches for investors.

D. diversity: Investing in technology companies and emerging industries can aid investors seeking to build a well-rounded portfolio. Because technology equities have little association with other traditional asset classes, they may offer the benefits of diversity and possibly reduced portfolio volatility.

2. Risks:

A. Market Volatility: Technology stocks and developing sectors are frequently susceptible to high levels of volatility due to factors like rapid advancements in technology, fluctuating investor sentiment, and ambiguous rules. Technology companies could see higher price fluctuations than other industries, which puts investors at risk, particularly those with shorter investment horizons.

B. Legal and Regulatory Risks: Emerging technologies, such as artificial intelligence and blockchain, are frequently subject to shifting legal and regulatory landscapes. Regulations, compliance demands, and legal matters that impact the financial success and future expansion of technology companies can increase investor risk.

C. Competition and Disruption: In the extremely competitive technology sector, existing businesses are constantly at risk from new entrants and innovative technologies. A technical company's competitive environment, market positioning, and ability to innovate and adapt are all important factors to take into account before investing.

D. Cybersecurity and Data Privacy: Data breaches and cybersecurity threats can affect digital platforms and technology companies, potentially resulting in financial losses, damage to their brand, and legal implications. Investors should assess a company's cybersecurity protocols and data privacy rules before making an investment to lessen the risk of cyber catastrophes.

E. Technological Obsolescence: Investments in some industries may become obsolete or replaced by more recent developments since emerging technologies, including blockchain and artificial intelligence, are continually evolving. An investor in a technological company should carefully consider R&D projects, industry trends, and the company's ability to innovate and adapt over the long run.

In summary, investing in technology companies, digital platforms, and emerging industries like blockchain and artificial intelligence (AI) presents opportunities for growth and innovation, but it also carries risks including market volatility, regulatory uncertainty, competitiveness, cybersecurity, and technological obsolescence. Investing in the rapidly evolving and dynamic world of technology carries risks, thus it is important for investors to diversify their holdings, assess risk, and conduct thorough due diligence.

To build a diversified investment portfolio that guards against downside risks and capitalises on digital trends, meticulous planning, thorough research, and astute asset allocation are required. This thorough guide will help you create a balanced portfolio that capitalizes on emerging digital trends:

1. **Establish Your Investing Objectives and Risk Tolerance:** Prioritize setting your investing goals, risk tolerance, and time horizon. Find out if you want to invest for long-term growth, income, or a combination of the two. It's important to assess how comfortable you are with potential losses and market volatility.

2. **Identify Digital Trends and Themes:** Get to know the digital media themes and trends that are driving innovation and the economy. Investigate emerging technologies, industries, and companies including blockchain, e-commerce, cloud computing, fintech, and digital healthcare

to identify investment opportunities that match your financial goals and risk tolerance.

3. **Identify Investment Possibilities:** To identify specific investment opportunities, thoroughly research digital trends and subjects. Look for companies that have a strong base, a competitive advantage, innovative products or services, and room to grow. Consider a mix of investments in mid-cap growing companies, promising startups, and well-established technology leaders to diversify your exposure across various risk profiles and development phases.

4. **Allocate Capital Strategically:** To create a diversified portfolio, distribute your capital strategically throughout several asset classes, industries, and regions. Consider combining stocks, bonds, real estate, and alternative assets in your portfolio to diversify risk and increase its

resilience. Invest in a variety of digital trends and subjects based on their risk-return profile, growth potential, and degree of correlation with other assets.

5. **Diversify Across Market Segments and Industries:** In the digital economy, diversify your portfolio across market segments and industries to lower the risk of concentration and to take advantage of opportunities in other industries. To reduce downside risks and improve portfolio stability, balance your exposure to high-growth industries like technology, e-commerce, and fintech with more defensive industries like healthcare and consumer staples.

6. **Examine ETFs and Mutual Funds:** Exchange-traded funds (ETFs) and mutual funds offer diverse portfolios of stocks, bonds, and other assets that give investors exposure to digital trends and themes. To obtain focused exposure to digital themes

while enjoying the advantages of professional management and risk diversification, look for thematic exchange-traded funds (ETFs) or sector-specific funds that emphasize technology, innovation, and disruptive movements.

7. **Observe and make adjustments Frequently:** To keep your intended asset allocation and risk profile, periodically review your investment portfolio and make adjustments as necessary. Review your investing thesis, the state of the market, and the performance of your portfolio on a regular basis to look for areas where you can reallocate or make modifications. Rebalancing ensures that over time, your portfolio stays in line with your investing objectives and risk tolerance.

8. **Remain Educated and Flexible:** Remain up to date on industry advancements,

emerging technologies, and legislative modifications that could affect your investment holdings. Keep an eye on how digital trends and themes are changing all the time, and be ready to modify your investment plan as necessary to take advantage of new opportunities and reduce risk.

Through adherence to these guidelines and the use of a methodical approach to the creation and administration of investment portfolios, you can develop a diversified investment portfolio that leverages digital trends while reducing possible negative consequences. To successfully traverse the complexity of digital investing, keep in mind to be patient, disciplined, and focused on your long-term financial objectives. You should also seek professional guidance when necessary.

Chapter 6: Safeguarding Your Electronic Resources

In today's increasingly digital world, protecting your digital assets is crucial to preventing data breaches, cyberattacks, and other security risks. The best practices and crucial tactics for safeguarding your digital assets—such as bank accounts, online personas, and personal data—are covered in this chapter. Learn how to strengthen your defences and reduce the hazards that come with living in the digital era, from cybersecurity measures to privacy protection.

In the contemporary digital era, cybersecurity and data privacy are becoming serious concerns for individuals and organisations alike. In the era of growing cyber dangers, protecting your online accounts and personal data is essential to avoiding data breaches, identity theft, and financial fraud. This section describes the importance of cybersecurity and data privacy and provides useful tips on how to protect online accounts, avoid online threats, and identify fraudulent activity.

1. **<u>Understanding the Importance of Cybersecurity and Data Privacy:</u>**

- Cybersecurity is the process of shielding computer systems, networks, and data from unauthorized access, cyberattacks, and data breaches.

- Data privacy is the process of preventing unauthorized use, access, or disclosure of private or sensitive information.

- Cybersecurity and data privacy are essential in the digital age to safeguard people's financial assets, online identities, and personal information from hackers and other malicious actors.

2. **Helpful Tips for Protecting Online Accounts:**

- **Use Robust Passwords:** Instead of using easily guessed information, offer each online account a unique, complex password. Consider utilising a password manager in order to generate and securely store strong passwords.

- **Activate Two-Factor Authentication (2FA):** Whenever possible, enable 2FA to further secure your online accounts. In most cases, a code or confirmation is provided in this manner via an additional device or app.

- **Maintain Software Updates:** Make sure you regularly update your operating system, security software, and web browser to protect yourself against known vulnerabilities and exploits.

- **Beware of Phishing Schemes:** Exercise caution when clicking links or opening attachments in unsolicited emails or texts. Be wary of phishing attempts that pose as trustworthy websites or companies.

- **Safeguard Your Wi-Fi Network:** Make sure your home network has strong encryption and a strong password to prevent unauthorized access. Regularly update the firmware on your router and turn off remote administration.

3. **Protecting Yourself From Online Threats:**

- **Install Antivirus Software:** Make use of dependable antivirus software to detect and eliminate viruses, malware, and other harmful software from your devices.

- **Activate Firewall Protection:** Activate firewalls on your devices and network to stop unauthorized access and to keep an eye on and control all incoming and outgoing network traffic.

- **Use Secure Connections:** When transmitting or viewing private information online or visiting sensitive websites, be sure the connection is secured using a virtual private network (VPN) or HTTPS.

- Adopt safe online habits by avoiding clicking on suspicious links, obtaining data from shady sources, and visiting malicious websites. Restrict the quantity of private information you share on social media platforms and exercise caution when sharing it.

4. Locating and Reporting Fraudulent Incidents:

- **Keep an eye on account behavior:** Make sure to regularly review your bank and credit card statements to look for any odd or questionable activity. Notify your bank as soon as possible if there are any discrepancies.

- **Review your credit record.** Watch your credit report closely for any signs of fraudulent activity or identity theft. Report any inaccuracies or strange activity to the credit reporting bureaus.

- **Keep Up to Date:** You may stay informed on the most recent cybersecurity threats and scams by subscribing to reputable news sources, cybersecurity blogs, government agencies, and news websites. Inform the appropriate authorities about any shady emails, texts, or websites.

By following the suggestions in this article and adopting a proactive approach to cybersecurity and data privacy, you can protect your digital assets and reduce the likelihood that you will become a victim of financial fraud, identity theft, and cyberattacks. Stay vigilant, keep your software and security measures up to date, and educate yourself on new threats and safe online privacy and security practices.

Since insurance products offer assistance and financial protection in the event of identity theft, cyber incidents, and other cybercrimes, they are crucial for safeguarding financial assets against cyber risks. Two crucial insurance products that could decrease the financial impact of digital dangers are cyber insurance and identity theft protection.

1. **Defence Against Theft of Identity:**

- Identity theft protection insurance can help families and individuals financially recover from losses and damages due to identity theft.

- This type of insurance typically pays for lost wages, legal fees, credit monitoring, and identity restoration services, among other expenses related to identity theft.

- Insurance against identity theft can help victims of identity theft get through the challenging process of repairing their credit history, restoring their identity, and disputing unfounded allegations.

- Certain identity theft protection plans also incorporate proactive measures like credit monitoring and identity theft alerts to help spot suspicious behaviour and stop identity theft before it happens.

2. **Cyberspace Insurance:**

- Cyber insurance can provide businesses with security and financial support in the event of cyberattacks, data breaches, and other cyber incidents.

- Cyber insurance policies typically cover a range of costs associated with cyber disasters, such as forensic investigations, data recovery and restoration, legal bills, regulatory fines and penalties, and notification expenses.

- Cyber insurance may also cover liability claims stemming from data breaches or privacy violations, business disruption expenses, and ransomware payments to hackers.

- Plans for cyber insurance offer configurable coverage options and restrictions to manage the unique cyber risks that different industries and companies face. They can be modified to meet the specific needs and risk tolerance of a company.

The significance of insurance products such as cyber insurance and identity theft protection in safeguarding financial assets against cyber risks cannot be overstated. By providing individuals and businesses with financial security and a safety net in the event of identity theft and cyber disasters, these insurance policies seek to mitigate the potentially disastrous financial repercussions of digital hazards.

By purchasing extensive insurance coverage and putting proactive cybersecurity measures in place, people and organisations may protect their financial assets and lessen the risks associated with functioning in an increasingly digital environment.

Chapter 7: Making Future Plans

Future planning is necessary to achieve long-term financial success and stability. This chapter covers the major components of financial planning as well as investing strategies for building wealth and achieving financial goals, retirement planning, and estate planning. Discover how to create a comprehensive financial plan that can provide you the confidence and peace of mind you need to tackle life's obstacles. Everything from goal-setting and budgeting to asset diversification and life-uncertainty planning will be covered in this plan.

Strategies for Long-Term Financial Planning in the Digital Age and Retirement Savings:

1. **Set Financial Goals:**

To start, decide on your desired retirement age, expected level of living, and anticipated retirement expenses. These are important financial goals for your retirement. Use digital technology to quantify these goals and track your progress over time.

2. **Automate Savings and Investing:**

Use automated savings software to schedule recurring transfers from your checking account to an investment portfolio or retirement savings account. Saving money is made simple with apps like Acorns, Digit, and Qapital that round up purchases or allow you to set aside a portion of your earnings.

- **Consider robo-advisors if you'd like** to use automated investment management.

These web-based resources create and manage a variety of investment portfolios based on your risk tolerance, financial goals, and time horizon. Among these are Ellevest, Wealthfront, and Betterment.

- **Use Retirement Accounts that Offer Tax Benefits:** The maximum amount of money can be contributed to tax-advantaged retirement plans, such as 401(k)s, Roth IRAs, and IRAs. Make use of employer-sponsored retirement plans, and consider contributing enough, if available, to qualify for company matching contributions.

- **To ensure that your assets are in line** with your risk tolerance and long-term financial goals, monitor them and make any required adjustments. To maintain desired asset proportions, many robo-advisors offer automated portfolio rebalancing.

3. **Make Use of Resources for Online Retirement Planning:**

- Utilise online retirement planning tools and calculators to assess your readiness for retirement, project your future retirement income needs, and determine whether you're on pace to meet your goals. Resources such as Personal Capital, Fidelity's Retirement Score, and Vanguard's Retirement Nest Egg Calculator are important sources of information.

- You can estimate your sources of retirement income, evaluate withdrawal strategies, and budget for healthcare expenses in retirement by using the retirement planning calculators offered by financial institutions.

4. **Continue to Learn and Stay Informed:**

- Make sure you stay informed about changes to tax laws, retirement plans, and investing trends by following reputable blogs, podcasts, and sources for financial news. By keeping up with market developments and pursuing further information, you will be able to make informed judgements and adjust your retirement plan as needed.

5. **Seek Professional Advice When Needed:** It's essential to consult a financial advisor or planner if you need specific advice on retirement planning techniques or if your financial circumstances are complicated. A knowledgeable advisor can help you navigate the challenges of retirement planning in the digital era and provide recommendations that are tailored to your own circumstances.

Giving people the tools they need to take control of their financial futures is crucial in the present digital world. Using cutting-edge tools and platforms, people may more effectively optimise their retirement goals, assets, and savings. The following advice can be used to safeguard readers' cash when utilising technology:

1. **Automate Savings and Investing:**

Use automated savings apps and programmes like Acorns, Digit, or Qapital to set up automatic transfers from your checking account to savings or investing accounts. These apps analyse your buying patterns and automatically set away little amounts to make saving easy.

Take a look at robo-advisors such as Wealthfront or Betterment, which employ computers to create and oversee investment portfolios according to your financial goals and risk tolerance. They automate investment decisions and portfolio rebalancing, making investing simple and accessible.

2. Keep an eye on your spending and budget:

To monitor your finances, make spending goals, and keep track of your expenditures, use budgeting software like Mint or PocketGuard. These apps categorise your spending, offer details about your financial habits, and offer customised cost-cutting recommendations.

Make use of the online banking features offered by your bank or lending institution to keep an eye on transactions, set spending caps, and receive real-time alerts for unusual activity. Many banks offer tools and dashboards to help you manage your money effectively.

3. Enhance Your Retirement Strategy:

Use the widely available online retirement planning tools and calculators to assess your readiness for retirement, forecast your future income requirements, and identify any gaps in your retirement funds. Websites like Personal Capital and Vanguard offer retirement planning tools that evaluate your financial situation and provide helpful guidance.

Consider opening individual retirement accounts (IRAs) or signing up for employer-sponsored retirement plans such as 401(k)s in order to effectively prepare for retirement taxes. Many companies offer retirement planning tools and services to help employees make educated decisions about their retirement savings.

4. **Continue to Learn and Stay Informed:**

To stay up to date on investing trends, retirement planning strategies, and financial news, make use of podcasts, newsletters, and online resources. Keep up with the latest happenings in the financial world by subscribing to reliable blogs, social media platforms, and financial websites.

To enhance your knowledge of personal finance, investing concepts, and retirement planning techniques, take advantage of the webinars, seminars, and online courses that are provided by financial institutions, investment businesses, or educational platforms.

Readers may be proactive and use technology to optimise retirement plans, investments, and savings in order to save money and build wealth for the future. By utilising digital tools and platforms, people may streamline money management, make informed decisions, and ultimately take control of their financial futures.

In summary, the digital era presents never-before-seen chances for people to take control of their financial futures. Readers may more easily and effectively than ever before optimize their retirement goals, investments, and savings by using technology. Digital planning platforms, robo-advisors, and automated technologies all provide tremendous assistance by simplifying procedures and providing insightful data.

But it's important to keep in mind that technology is a tool, not a replacement for sound financial management and knowledge. Digital tools may make money management easier, but in the end, discipline, well-defined financial objectives, and well-informed decision-making are what will determine success.

May readers use technology responsibly, be educated, and be proactive in pursuing their financial goals as they set out on their financial journeys in the digital age. They may successfully manage the intricacies of the financial world and achieve long-term financial stability and prosperity if they are committed, prudent, and have access to the correct tools.

www.ingramcontent.com/pod-product-compliance
Lightning Source LLC
Chambersburg PA
CBHW071213240526
45470CB00018B/1859